MW00620922

1

DISCLAIMER

Though the author originally went to college for Psychology she never became a Psychologist. The trajectory of life allowed her to receive her degree in Communications, hence this lovely book you are about to read. The advice contained in this material might not be suitable for everyone. The author designed the information to present her opinion about the subject matter. The reader must carefully investigate all aspects of self before committing him or herself to receiving their intended call back. The author obtained the information contained herein from her very own life experiences, self-reflection, and lessons she has learned over time. She neither implies nor intends any guarantee of similar results. The author is not in the business of giving mental, emotional, or any other type of professional advice. Should the reader need such advice, he or she must seek services from a competent professional. The author particularly disclaims any liability, loss, or risk taken by individuals who directly or indirectly act on the information contained herein. The author believes the advice presented here is sound, but readers cannot hold her responsible for either the actions they take or the risk taken by individuals who directly or indirectly act on the information contained herein.

Published by The Chic Inspirational Publishing Co.

A division of The Callback, LLC

Printed in the United States

Cover design by Cedric Morris

Book design and production by Talookah Studio

Author photograph by Brene Ashley

Editing by Rachel Arterberry

Copyright © 2020 by Jontice Tanae

ISBN 978-0-578-57591-9

INTRODUCTION

Have you ever been in a quarter-life crisis? You know, that moment in your twenties when life is driving full speed, with no direction, and at any moment it feels as if you will have a fatal crash! Whenever I use the term "quarter-life crisis," people chuckle at the thought of twenty somethings having enough issues in life to identify with a crisis. The Collins Dictionary defines quarter-life crisis as "a crisis that may be experienced in one's twenties, involving anxiety over the direction, and quality of one's life."

My quarter-life crisis seemed to begin just as I threw my graduation cap into the air and kissed my undergraduate studies goodbye! As I pranced off the stage with my fancy degree, I just knew all my dreams were on their way to becoming my reality. I imagined myself with a super successful job to match my studies, a steady relationship with the love of my life, on the road to be being married, and birthing beautiful babies to carry on my legacy.

I'm sure life as we know it found my overly eager imagination quite hilarious. Here I was in my early to mid-twenties working as a receptionist—a position I absolutely dreaded. Which was followed by a whirlwind of relationship turmoil, being constantly on an emotional roller coaster with my boyfriend that ended in his cheating. Talk about the ultimate betrayal, I mean really, the nerve of him. After all we had been through.

Such mishaps certainly landed me a face-plant on rock bottom. This was by far the lowest I had ever been in my life. Depression and I became best friends. I cried every day for what felt like forever. I found myself low and unwilling to make an effort to take control of my life. Then one day, I glanced up at the mirror and decided enough was enough. I refused to continue to accept the path I was on and knew that a change had to come. The time had come for me to take matters into my own hands.

In that moment, I learned that if I wanted different results, I had to start by doing things differently. I made a conscious decision to go on a fast from social media, redirect my focus, and apply for a minimum of 20 jobs per week. About two weeks into the fast and hard-core job search, emails from prospective employers began to come in. The results from my practice were unbelievable. I was setting up interviews more frequently than I could possibly imagine. For six weeks straight, I went on an average of three interviews per week. It was one of the most exciting and nerve-racking moments I had ever encountered so far. It was definitely an experience for the books (pun intended).

About two months in, I began to realize I was at the be-ginning of my breakthrough. The audacity of life to give me this hand and expect me to fail. I wanted a change for myself. I deserved better in all aspects of my life. I took these sour lemons that life gave me and began to make lemonade. I wanted better so I went after better.

I finally decided to leave that cheating guy alone and started dating. After going on dates with different guys from various backgrounds over a relatively short period of time, I began to notice something quite interesting.

When interviewing for a job, frequently my routine was to research the potential employers, stalk LinkedIn profiles, and practice behavioral interview questions. With dating, it was the exact same process. Instead of doing a Google search on the dating candidate, I did a Case search (a database that provides public access to the case records of the State Judiciary using first and last names); and stalked Instagram and Twitter pages. And instead of simulating interviews to practice behavioral interview questions, I called my girlfriends to dissect and discuss text messages sent to whomever I was dating or considering dating.

Funny and weird as it may sound, through this time of my life I realized that interviewing was very similar to dating! Having been exposed to the good and bad of both dating and interviewing, I found them to be equally exciting and yet, stressful.

They have helped me learn so much about myself; how to love myself, to make decisions for myself, and to accept myself, flaws and all. As I approach the end of a decade, moving into my thirties, I realize how the lessons I learned in my twenties have ultimately shaped and transitioned me. What was once the biggest TEST in this stage of life has now become my biggest TESTIMONY.

If you are looking to shift from breakdown to break-through in this chapter of your life and are wondering when you will get "the callback," I encourage you to read ahead.

TABLE OF CONTENTS

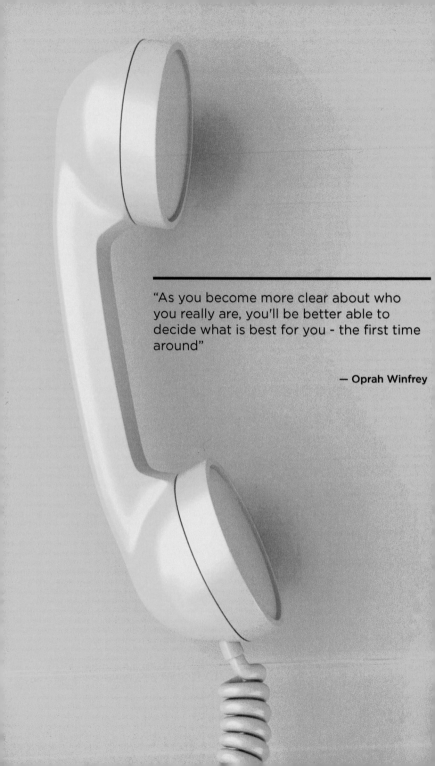

"As you become more clear about who you really are, you'll be better able to decide what is best for you - the first time around"

— Oprah Winfrey

Chapter 1
Let's be Clear

Believe it or not, being clear on what you want can and will save you from a lot. When I look at the people around me and compare their dating encounters, I find it unique how people from older generations get into serious relationships faster than people in younger generations. I have witnessed situations where marriages lasted for 25+ years after six months of dating in their late twenties/early thirties, and other marriages that failed after six years of dating when the relationship began during their teenage years. I don't believe age is the key to success in these relationships, but I do believe maturity, learning from previous experiences, and being clear on what you want is.

In the dating world, knowing what you want out of the deal is as equally important as it is in any other circumstance. Understand, people will try to project their fears on you. Do not let them. It is easy to fear the unknown and live according to society's expectation. Live the best life YOU can envision for yourself.

Now . . . since I have clearly stated that, let me tell you a story.

As a teenager my parents always preached to me not to get caught up in relationships, so I never did. This was something hard to accept and process, but I tried to do as I was told. I always had some kind of companionship, but never anything too official.

About six months after that monumental graduation moment, I met my newest interest. There was this new guy at my job. He was so handsome and had just the cutest smile. After random stare contests and very irrelevant conversations with him, I was super curious to see what he was about. Even though he shared his M&M's with me, I was still too shy to approach him, so I called one of my good girlfriends (GGF) for help.

My GGF was more than excited to get the scoop on him. She was that ideal friend who wanted what was best for you, so she was going to ask all you needed to know to make sure it would be a good fit. I knew I chose the perfect person to get the scoop, so I was excited to see how her investigation went.

Days went by, and my GGF and I were finally having one of our famous "catch-up" conversations, she was excited to reveal what she found out about this new guy. The conversation was going great and she told me everything I needed to know. I was so excited to hear about all the juicy information on my new "friend" and then the bomb drops. "…but yea girl, he 18 but he will be 19 soon." My heart skipped a beat as I clenched my chest. All I could do was shake my head in disbelief. I knew it was too good to be true. Remind you, I had just graduated college. I was GROWN grown. She told me he was 18 as if it were the legal drinking age. I was soooo confused. LOL!

First of all, what the hell was my GGF thinking?! Not only did she come back to report that he was 18, she is persistent that I pursue him. I don't think I have ever been so puzzled in my entire life (I was still in my "excited to go to Happy Hour because I could drink legally phase").

But then again, all I could think about was his cute ill' smile, and how he shared his M&M's with me, and everything girlfriend reported back to me was actually good information. He was indeed younger than I but had so much going on to be barely legal. Honestly, he was doing better than me as a college graduate. He was working full- time; I was only working part-time. He was living with a roommate, and I was scraping up money to pay my mother rent for the same bedroom I grew up in. The only downfall was he was younger than me. In fact, he was younger than me living a more adult life than I was. Ultimately, I gave in and decided to think about it.

A week later, "Smiley," as I affectionately called him, and I had a conversation. He put two and two together and realized I was the friend that he was recently being interrogated for. Our conversation continued and he explained to me he was a man, made me chuckle, and that he would like to take me out. I was hesitant at first, but then I thought, "What could I lose from going on a date?" A free meal is always desirable. Needless to say, he eventually became my boyfriend, best friend, and unfortunately, worst enemy. Before Smiley and I made things official, there were many jokes about me dating someone younger than myself. I didn't care because it was what I wanted, and I was clear of that. A companion who was about having a good time, not nothing exclusive. He was just that. If I wasn't breaking any legal or moral rules, everything was fair game.

What if I had decided to go after a guy who was ready to settle down at the time? I am pretty sure I would be divorced right now, or in an unstable/unhealthy toxic marriage (worst case scenario). I was not ready to settle down or be serious. I was at a point in my life that if I had, I would have hurt somebody and become damaged goods within my own mess. But hear me out. I am not saying that getting married young creates that environment. But for me, in my early twenties, chile please. I barely had a job. Let me clarify. I barely had a "real" job. I partied more than I slept, and I was still trying to figure out my purpose. No way was I thinking about being serious with anybody. I was barely serious for my own good. To be serious for somebody else was a definite no-no.

Fresh out of college, I had no true understanding of handling finances or how to make a home-cooked meal, let alone possess society's definition of wife or girlfriend qualities. So, I did what I wanted and took the young man up on his offer. It was fun while it lasted. I learned so much about myself and the qualities that I desired in a man. If it weren't for me knowing what I wanted then, I would be dating for purposes that exceeded me. I would be dating for qualities that other women wanted, which are probably things I could give a damn about. Knowing what I wanted and going after it showed me who I am, what I desire, and inspired me to never care about anyone's opinion about my life. At the end of the day, I created many enjoyable moments and lessons.

That relationship was the introduction of the woman I am evolving into. I was exposed to the good, the bad, and the ugly of myself. I learned my non-negotiables and saw firsthand what I could tolerate and what I couldn't.

This same lesson was learned as I was interning. In the earlier stages of my career, I did a lot of free work. I had two unpaid internships as well as voluntary freelance work. I did all of this while working two part-time jobs. During my juggle days, I recall my mother telling me to switch career fields. For the life of her, she couldn't understand the significance of working for free. The reality is, it was not meant for her to understand. One of the hardest lessons while transitioning to an adult is setting boundaries with your parents. They want the best for you. While that is appreciated and respected, they also have to learn and respect they raised you to become the best version of yourself, and the only way to see that through is to let you have the opportunity to make decisions for yourself. It is not easy, but you have to get comfortable having those uncomfortable conversations. It sucks but it is worth it, and it is the best for your success and growth. Your parents want to protect you, and for that we will love them forever, but they cannot protect us from who we are destined to be. With our destiny we may fail but with failure you have two options: and that is, to lose or learn.

The choice is yours.

At that time of my internships, my main focus was on two things; opportunity and exposure. I was hungry for it and did not care where it was coming from. I knew my heart's desires and was determined to do whatever it took to fulfill them. Working for free gave me gratitude that I still carry with me as I transition throughout my career. Not only has my past internships made me grateful, I am also humble, and I have a growing network of contacts that know and appreciate me for working for free while putting my best foot forward. My internships laid the foundation for my ever-growing career path. Years later, I can still refer back to skills and opportunities learned which helped me get where I am today. I love my mother more than anybody on this planet, but I could not let her, or anyone else's projections, deter me from going after the goals I set for myself. I was clear on my goals and aspirations. Accomplishing goals brought me joy, and that's what I was going to continue to do.

Figuring out what brings you joy is not the easiest thing to do, which is why it is very important to learn to listen to your inner self. You have to learn to hear your voice while ensuring you are tuning out everyone else. Only you can decide what is best for you. And you are the only person who has to make sure that what is best for you, happens to you. Never let any projections, rumors, or fears of others stop you from going after what you want.

Make sure you get in tune with yourself. Don't be afraid to dine alone at your favorite restaurant or purchase a movie ticket for one. Learn to love yourself. As a human being, it is natural to want the presence of another person, but make sure the decisions you make are based on your inner thoughts and not fulfilling temporary emotions. The biggest battle is usually your heart versus your mind, or your thoughts versus your emotions. The mind knows what is best. Your emotions are temporary and will change.

Always go with your thought process.

When I finally decided to let go of my previous relationship, I had an insightful conversation with one of my male friends. He reminded me that I was a wonderful person and that it was time for me to focus on me. In that moment, I was annoyed with him because I believed I was already focused on me. I was truly insulted. He told me to take some time to Netflix and chill by myself, read a book, and just focus on key components that I believe make me a great person. Looking back on that very moment, I now understand the message he was trying to convey. Once I gained peace with myself, I never lost another piece of myself. It was in my alone time that I realized and accepted that I am the wonderful person I was often told I am, and even through pain I am still evolving to a better me. I had to be clear with me again in order to start my next chapter.

I challenge you to take some time for yourself and actually fall in love with yourself. Understand that loving yourself and implementing strategies in your life to promote self-love are different. I am pretty sure you love yourself and your confidence is through the roof. To love yourself is not the hard part, it is the work of loving yourself that's complicated. The practice of self- love and self-care should be done daily for maximum results.

Once you enter the routine of adulting it is so easy to forget to put yourself first. You wake up, get ready for work, go to work, get off work, come home, get ready for bed, then repeat. It is only that simple if you are single with no kids or other major responsibilities. It seems as though the more responsibilities, you have the less time you have to make for yourself. Adulting is a huge scam.

Our routines are distractions and often times prevent us from practicing efficient self-care habits. Trying some minor changes can make a major impact like taking some time off from social media and putting your phone on the charger and really enjoying a movie. I often find my most peaceful moments when I come home from work, water Peaches (my bamboo plant), and just sit on my couch in silence. In these quiet moments, I am able to redirect my focus, acknowledge my flaws and wrongdoings, and set new plans and goals to move forward in life. This is where everything becomes clear and I am able to move with intention. I am far from perfect, but my experiences have molded me, and I strive to not have to go through the same trials again simply because I didn't learn my lesson the first go-around.

I have included some tips for you on how to determine what you want and how to go after it:

1. Make a vision board.

• Look through magazines and cut out words, phrases, and pictures of things you want to accomplish in life.

• Place your cut outs on a board.

• Set the board in a location where you will see it often.

The brain is a powerful instrument. Feed it and watch it work in your favor.

The subconscious mind holds on to goals that the conscious mind dismisses, but still gives us the push we need to fulfill our goals. It's a different kind of enlightenment, and I love it. I have made vision boards in the past and have been successful in achieving my dreams and goals.

One of the most important tasks I like to do before and after I make the board is to pray over it. Personally, I like for my professional goals to align with my spiritual goals.

2. Write out your goals.

Your short-term goals should be a series of events that lead to your long-term goals.

Write them out, make them realistic, challenge yourself, and strive for them daily. Make sure you write them out. Don't take a mental note. There is something about being clear on your goals and having them on paper. It's as if you are setting up an alignment to allow greatness to come into your life.

3. Reflect on your experiences.

Reflect on the good, the bad, and the ugly. Get a journal and write it down. Compare experiences from days, months, or years ago. It is in your reflection that you should become clear on what you want, what you will tolerate, and what you will not.

4. Don't be afraid to talk to strangers.

This is a twist. Strangers are often the best people to receive insight from because they offer an unbiased, honest perspective. Think about it. Someone who doesn't know you usually wouldn't walk on eggshells in a conversation with you because they don't know your triggers.

The words "talk to a stranger" may sound creepy because children are usually taught not to. But we are adults now and it's not as dangerous.

During your next ride-sharing experience, don't be afraid or too antisocial to engage with your driver, hope- fully a seasoned, married person. They may be in a position to offer some sound advice about marriage that may help on your next date or you may receive some new life tips.

When you get a new connection on LinkedIn, shoot your shot and ask for an informational interview (an informal conversation) from the person who currently holds your dream title. There are many benefits in informational interviews and you never know what kind of doors it may open for you.

5. Accept yourself for who you are.

You have to fall in love with yourself daily, flaws and all. If you embrace your flaws, no one will ever be able to use them against you. With social media being so prevalent, it is easy to compare ourselves to others. However, comparison is the thief of joy. Speak affirmations to your- self daily. Look in the mirror and remind yourself who you are.

And if you have forgotten, repeat after me.

"I AM BEAUTIFUL. I AM STRONG. I AM CLEAR AND UNDERSTAND THAT WHERE I AM TODAY IS EXACTLY WHERE I AM SUPPOSED TO BE NO MATTER WHAT MISTAKES I MADE YESTERDAY!"

CHAPTER 1 | ACTIVITY:

Have you ever taken the time to write out the specifics you desire whether it is in your relationships (intimate and platonic), job, business, personal, or anything you may be focused on at the current moment?

In the space provided write out your intentions and be extremely clear and detailed.

Or if you are a visual person use the space provided to create a vision board. You can draw pictures, write words, or cut out words and pictures from magazines to have your dreams on paper.

Have fun! Think BIG

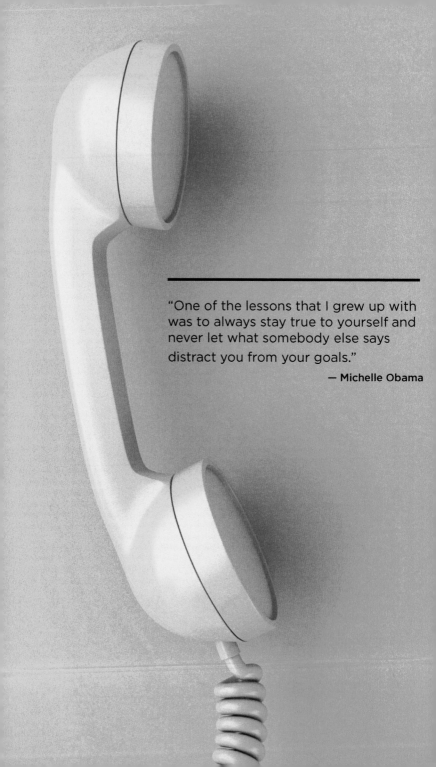

"One of the lessons that I grew up with was to always stay true to yourself and never let what somebody else says distract you from your goals."

— Michelle Obama

Chapter 2
Keep it Real

During my season of interviewing and dating, I realized how fake I can be. When I prepared for interviews, I found myself making up scenarios to common behavioral questions. And during my preparation for first dates, I chose to solicit different perspectives and opinions on random "what-if" situations from social media. It is so amazing how in these imperative moments that have the biggest impact on our lives, we send our representatives instead of being our true selves. When we try to act "perfect" for the situation, we tend to end up in situations we do not want. What's for you will be for you. Be in the position to accept what's honestly for you. You can only do that by keeping it real…with yourself.

Have you ever felt like you wanted something you knew you weren't ready to receive? Have you ever sat and wondered what your day-to-day activities would include as a CEO, but you're currently in an entry-level position? Or you imagined life as a stay-at-home mom with no children, or coming home to do wifey duties and you are not dating? Sometimes our thoughts and imagination get the best of us. And that is okay. If you believe it will happen, it will. When this happens, I believe there is something internally reminding me I am more than what I am settling for, and it is time to put myself in the position to go after what I want. If you find yourself in this case, utilize your resources to make yourself qualified for the position. Don't ever doubt yourself. If you feel something is out of your league, boss up and get the necessary qualifications to join the "league," then act accordingly. Whatever you set your sights on is certainly obtainable, and you may already have the skills required. You just have to find a way to let it out and let it show. Be comfortable with yourself and never leave your confidence at home. Even Beyoncé had to start somewhere.

Make your intentions clear and do not be fearful.

This is why being clear on what you want is so necessary. You can use what you have to get what you want. When you are your true self, the things and people you desire come to you.

When in search of a job, prospective candidates typically submit resumes for positions they believe they qualify for and would like to interview for. Resumes include key words and phrases to demonstrate how we have excelled or exceeded expectations in education and/or previous positions held. When trying to entice an employer to call us for an interview, we often glamorize the work we have done for other people, forgetting what makes us good in our positions. The difference between you and any other applicant are your interpersonal skills or the soft skills you possess and bring to the table. If you are a "people person," do not be afraid to let it show. There are many skills that can be taught, but how to interact with someone in a harmonious way is not one of them. Let that charismaticness shine bright. If you are the most organized person you know and treat organization like a science, do just that. Your resume should include ALL relevant skills you possess including your soft skills because your soft skills are what make you uniquely you. Show your passion. Demonstrate all of the great qualities that you have, those that make you who you were created to be, and how those amazing qualities will be an asset to the company you are applying to.

Let's compare the resume process to the dating world: whether you are out scouting, or swiping left or right, keep in mind the same attitude as if you were preparing your resume. Don't sell yourself short. If nobody has told you today, let me be the first to remind you that you are wonderful and great. Be just that and nothing less.

Take some time to look within yourself and recognize your good personality traits. If you are having a hard time figuring out what they are, ask a trusted friend or loved one what are their favorite qualities they like about you. To make this more interesting, ask what is their least favorite too. Constructive criticism is healthy and assists us in becoming better. Once you know these things, take time to nurture these qualities by capitalizing on your strengths and working to improve your weaknesses. In order to receive this criticism, you have to be in an honest state, or your insecurities will make you defensive instead of being in a position to receive. Do not take things too personally when being criticized and accept that no one is perfect. Therefore, the people around you that love and care for you, will tell you about yourself to better yourself. You have to be real with yourself to accept that you have flaws. After you accept your flaws, you are able to move in a better direction and evolve into a better version of yourself.

THE CALL BACK

During a phone interview or in small talk, you have the opportunity to save yourself from a possibly horrible situation. Not all things are what they appear at first. From the job description you may have thought you had found the ultimate entry level position. Come to find out, the position actually requires you to knock on doors, begging people to purchase knives. Maybe you are physically attracted to a person based on their social media profile, but in conversation, you find out they are just a pretty or handsome face with no real values.

Once again, this is why it is imperative to know what you want before jumping into anything. If you are unsure, making a decision out of desperation will become the norm, and you will lose sight of your end goal. With this being said, try to think as rationally as possible. It is okay to give things a try. Every decision does not have to be made right now for the long term. But keep in mind, when you wear a mask or are not living in your truth, you receive those things that are deceptive of your true character.

Be authentic and you will receive authenticity.

During my season of interviewing, I found myself in a desperate state of mind. The worst part is that I didn't recognize it until it was pointed out to me during an interview, of all places. How embarrassing. To be called desperate is bad enough, let alone by a potential employer. I learned several valuable lessons from that interview. First, I had to accept that the statement was true. Then, I analyzed the facts. From the moment I walked through the doors, I knew that it was not a place for me, but I wanted to give it a fair shot. The environment was too quiet and there was not an ounce of humor in sight. The lighting was dark, the receptionist was not welcoming, and it was very quiet. You could honestly hear a pin drop.

I felt a stale, serious, and suspicious kind of vibe. I was so pressed for a new job that I ignored every red flag, and even my own intuition. (I am sure you have done this before.) Even while we were speaking, I could feel that the interviewer was having the same thoughts as I was. There was no real connection. The flow of the interview felt like an interrogation more than a conversation. There was a point where the interviewer asked a question about my experience, and I told him I have not done that yet but was willing to learn. That's when he told me I sounded desperate. We were not a perfect match and I was hoping and praying they would not request a callback. Close call, they didn't.

Right from the beginning it was proven I was lying to myself. I was so desperate at the time. Even though I knew from the start this was not the job for me, if given the opportunity, I would have accepted any offer they made. Low key, I hoped and prayed that they didn't call me back, but sort of kind of wished they did. I didn't like my current job, so I was willing to settle even though I knew better. I have done this while dating, too. Going from worse to bad just to fill a void. At the end of it all, I learned it was not worth it.

Don't allow your desperation to force your hand or go against what you know you want, or don't want. Let's say you are physically attracted to someone and you would like to get to know them, maybe through a phone call. As you would in any interview, you want to be the most alert during this first call. First impressions certainly go a long way, and any "first" can be very telling. With pen and paper ready, (mentally or literally) take note of everything going on. If the guy is talking about sex and you are celibate, do not stick around. If you know you want companionship with someone who is well-established, but all he talks about is how he "about to" do something with no plan or direction, don't stick around. Don't be afraid to ask questions. Don't be afraid to state your intentions. It is not common for someone to offer unsolicited information about themselves. If you don't ask, you will not know. Always, always, always ask questions. You don't want to come off as an investigator but ask your questions with a purpose. Remember, just like in a job interview, you want to learn as much about the "environment" and culture as possible. "Ignorance is bliss," so I have heard, but do not let the unknown keep you from living in your truth. Don't allow ignorance to be the reason you desperately try to fill a void. Pay attention and evaluate before moving forward.

"Fake it 'til you make it," they said. Honestly, this works. But it works and comes with a headache, if you have to lie or go out of your way for something—that is a clear indication that the opportunity is not for you.

In a recent interview one of my friends told me to lie on my resume. This friend also was going to go out of their way to be a reference for me. I considered telling the lie but decided against it. During the interview, I made it clear I was interested in the position but may not have had the background they were looking for. However, I was willing to learn and undergo any necessary trainings to become the best I could be. I was nervous because I knew it was possible that I was competing against others with more skills. But I also knew that if it were meant for me to get the job, it would have been mine. Nevertheless, I got the call back. Out of 14 candidates, little ol' me with no experience was hired. Months later I asked my boss how many people he had interviewed, and why did he choose me. He told me he saw the potential in me and knew that I would be a great asset to the company. He also reiterated that you can train any employee to get the job done but you cannot teach customer service or character. During my interview, I was my true self. I told jokes, expressed my interest, and made it clear my personality shines. I reiterated that I am a quick learner and open to learning new things. You can teach anyone the job, but you cannot teach personality, and because of that, I got the call back.

Keeping it real seems so easy to do, but so many don't. I believe many don't keep it real with others because they are not real with themselves. There is a huge lack of self-awareness in young adults. Adulting is hard. Transitioning to the person you believe you are destined to be is a lot of work, and takes a lot of time, honesty, patience and self- care.

We all have that friend (or we are that friend), who claims they don't want a relationship but tries to pursue every person they are dating. Friend (or self), you knew before you met that person, that you wanted something more meaningful and long-lasting. You didn't just wake up with those intentions. I am not saying that it's not possible to wake up with a change of heart, but you are not changing your heart every time you meet a new person. Face the facts, keep it real, and let's be clear on what you want.

Here's some tips to help you keep it real moving forward.

1. Don't be afraid to live in YOUR truth.

Whatever that means to you, especially if it is an unpopular opinion. You cannot be afraid to be you. Your perception is shaped from your experiences in life and you are entitled to it.

2. Be honest.

Honesty is the best policy. You can't keep it real if you are telling lies. It is harder to keep up with lies than it is to tell the truth. The truth never changes no matter how many times it is told. Lies—you have to keep up with them. Just tell the truth.

3. Set your intentions and make them clear.

If you do not know what your intentions are, take some time to unplug from the world and reflect. It is not a crime to journal and take notes of your feelings. When something makes you happy, take note; when something makes you sad, or mad, take note. This can help you process your emotions and shape your truest desires.

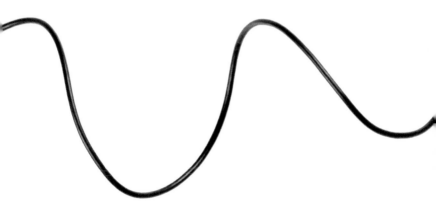

4. Don't be afraid to walk away.

If you are allowing something or someone who is against what you desire in your space, after you made it clear what your intentions are,

you are not being real with yourself. If it no longer serves you, then what is the purpose of having it in your life?

Now, repeat after me.

"I AM HONEST WITH MYSELF NO MATTER THE CIRCUMSTANCE."

CHAPTER 2 | ACTIVITY:

If you don't keep it real with yourself, you will never be able to keep it real with anything or anyone else.

What is one lie you have been living?

And what can you do to transition from living this lie to living in your truth?

Example: The lie I have been living is I am ok with growing my hair. I have been growing my hair out my entire life. It is annoying, it does not hold any styles, AND I do not know how to maintain it. I have tried everything. The only reason why I still have hair is because I am scared, I will not be attractive if I cut it. I will cut my hair little by little as I get comfortable with not having hair.

I will now live in my truth by:

Do you see what I did there? I have been living a lie and somebody else truth. I would constantly state how I do not like hair but still have a head full. Oh the contradictions. I realized the issue, told the real truth, and here I am bald and beautiful as can be.

Now is your turn. Let the truth set you free.

It is time to keep it real.

Your turn:

The lie I have been living is:

_____

_____

_____

_____

_____

_____

I will now live in my truth by:

_____

_____

_____

_____

_____

_____

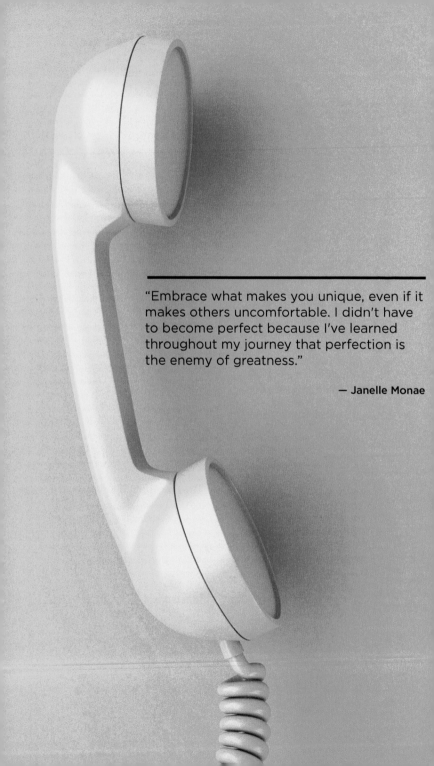

"Embrace what makes you unique, even if it makes others uncomfortable. I didn't have to become perfect because I've learned throughout my journey that perfection is the enemy of greatness."

— Janelle Monae

Chapter 3
Be You

The first "anything" always brings me so much anxiety. The thought of being excited makes me even more excited. It's weird and annoying, but it's joyful. The first thing I have to remember when on a first interview or date is don't think. Yep, I said it. Don't think. Well, don't think too much or you will think yourself into a rabbit hole. Once I get caught up in my thoughts, they take over and consume me. I have to allow myself to enter a place of relaxation and let the real me shine. I am pretty awesome in my most natural state if I do say so myself.

There is something about you that piqued the interest of the potential employer or love interest. Keep it up. Getting the interview or the phone call is the first step in the process. Now it is time to consider if you want to move forward, or not. Either way is good but get in the mood to clear things up for yourself.

Often people go on interviews and allow them to be one-sided. The entire interview process should revolve around each party getting what they want; you want the job, and they want a great employee. But you do not want any job you want a job that aligns with your goals, take advantage of this opportunity and ask questions. There is nothing worse than making a life-changing decision and not being certain of what you are getting yourself into. Be sure to communicate what is important to you; job or financial stability, exposure, opportunity, etc. Do not be afraid to communicate no matter how big or small something may seem. We all can deal with discomfort for some while but think about when a while is up.

The same rule applies when it comes to dating. As an undergrad, I remember having a class discussion about marriage in one of my Sociology classes. My professor immediately paused the conversation and told the class in a loud, aggressive, but informative tone, to make sure we always, always, always (yes, she said it three times) ask questions. She told us about her relationship with her husband who she had been married to for over 20 years. She reminded us repeatedly, that conversations and asking questions helped her learn about her husband, and for him to learn about her.

She finished her advice column for the day by saying, "If two people are not on the same page, how do you plan to move forward?" That has stuck with me ever since, and I make it a point to ask as many questions as possible when on a first date, while keeping the conversation interesting. Don't make it an interrogation but make it fun and worth your while. All questions don't have to get asked today. However, before the first date, know your deal breakers or nonnegotiables.

If you do not know what your deal breakers or nonnegotiables are, take some time to think about your ideal situation, and write out what it would be like. From there, write out what you absolutely can and cannot live without. Nothing is perfect and there are times where you have to compromise. A compromise is when you give up something to get something, finding a common ground where everyone is satisfied despite certain needs or wants not being met. What are some things you are not willing to compromise on? The qualities that are a hard yes, and a hard no, are your deal breakers. And not up for negotiation.

The majority of my first date experiences typically ended with an invitation for a second date. Now, if I decided to go on the second date or not, is up for discussion. There was a time when I was constantly going on first dates. Some of them were really fun but I refused to go on a second date with someone who I didn't see myself moving forward with. I don't want to waste your time nor mine, so I will do both of us a favor and cut things short. I do think I have always been invited back for another date because I am an enjoyable person. I have a strong, outgoing, sweet but aggressive, comical personality. I absolutely love it. It's what makes me ME. I also have a cute talent where I can make people laugh without intending to … I naturally allow this to show and shine.

In addition to my personality shining I try to put as much information on front street as I can. One situation in particular I thought I was being fair by letting my date know about one of my biggest flaws. Sleep and I are like two peas in a pod, especially after a couple of drinks. While out at a cute place to play miniature golf and have dinner and drinks within six minutes of our drive from the restaurant, I fell asleep mid conversation. To keep it real and state the facts, I told him this is a glimpse of what it is like to date me. I am always sleepy. Alcohol does not make this no better. I was comfortable telling him that, he deserved to know what he was getting himself into. He took it as though I was not interested. But in all actuality, I really am just tired. So maybe my sleepiness is not for everyone. I am perfectly okay with that.

As stated, some people will not know how to receive you and that is okay. If you are in a situation where you have to compromise who you are, then that situation is not for you.

During one of my many interviewing seasons, I was having a conversation with my mother. In her most judgmental tone she stated, "You out here applying for jobs, are you going to go on an interview like that?" She was referring to my platinum colored hair. Because "mothers know best," I was slightly offended. My anxiety got the best of me and had me reaching out to my friends that were human resource professionals, asking them if they judged people based on their hair color. I let fear get the best of me and considered buying a wig or dying my hair back to black. I was in a frenzy, until one day I was on Twitter and I saw a young lady mention that she recently went on a job interview with blue hair and told the employer she would dye her hair back if she needed to. The employer confirmed that it would not be necessary, and she got the job.

Her testimony was a friendly reminder that what is for you, will be for you, no matter the circumstances. I know my mother was trying to look out for me, but I also know that I cannot allow anyone's fears to be projected on me. I was confident in my process. I boldly interviewed for the jobs I really desired with true confidence knowing if it were meant for me, I would have it.

In another season of severe interviewing, out of four interviews, I received two job offers. With platinum hair I got The Callback twice. It was more than I expected. 50 percent isn't so bad when the odds are set up against you. I didn't have to change who I was to get what I wanted. And I am glad I didn't.

CHAPTER 3: BE YOU

1. If you have to change who you are for what you want, chances are it is not for you.

2. Never let fear stop you. If you are scared, channel that energy and become ambitious to chase your dream. You never know what you may be holding yourself from. Victory is on the other side of your fears.

3. Just because someone else tells you it might not be a good idea does not mean it is true. Do your own research and use your discernment for what is best for you.

4. Trust your gut. Your intuition will not steer you wrong. If you feel some type of way about something, trust your instincts. You are not feeling that way "just because."

5. Be you! You can't receive what's for you, if you are acting like someone else.

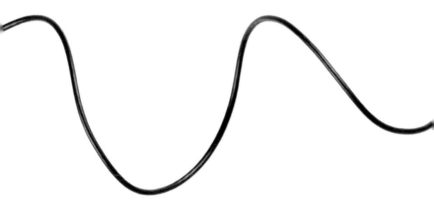

Bonus: Apply for that job. Send that DM. Shoot your shot. Remember you will miss 100% of the shots you don't take.

Now, repeat after me.

"I MAKE THIS PROMISE TO MYSELF: I WILL NOT CHANGE WHO I AM FOR ANYONE. IF YOU CAN'T RECEIVE ME AS ME, YOU DO NOT DESERVE ME OR MY ENERGY"

CHAPTER 3 | ACTIVITY:

Are you aware of your good, bad, and ugly? If you recognize and accept your flaws no one can use them against you. All of your characteristics whether you consider favorites or flawed makes you uniquely you and moving forward you should embrace it.

Using the example below complete the following questions.

I have a very smart mouth and some people take offense to it. My intent is never to offend others especially my loved ones. Moving forward I will take an additional 30 seconds to think before I speak and practice keeping some of my thoughts to myself. This is not about people feeling offended but more so about the way my message is being received after it is delivered.

Your Turn:

1. Acknowledge your short comings and decide can you do something about it. Then decide what you are going to do about it.

_____

_____

_____

_____

_____

2. Look at this from a different perspective. Is this flaw hindering me from what I desire? It is so easy to write things off as "this is just how I am." Let's practice being the change we want to see and rise to the occasion of practicing being better by changing for the better. (but only if YOU want to)

_____

_____

_____

_____

3. Embrace everything about you. Even if everyone thinks you have a bad attitude. It is your bad attitude, and nobody is forced to deal with it but you. Own everything about you. If you do not like it, fix it, but only fix it because you wanted to and not because you are people pleasing.

_____

_____

_____

_____

_____

_____

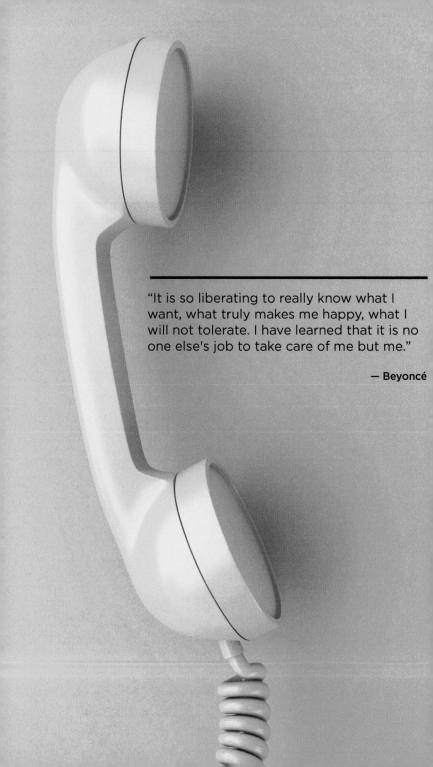

"It is so liberating to really know what I want, what truly makes me happy, what I will not tolerate. I have learned that it is no one else's job to take care of me but me."

— Beyoncé

Chapter 4
Make Lemonade

Now that you have been on your first date or interview and are waiting for the callback to schedule the second round or to move things forward, I am sure you are anxious and not really sure what to do. Just relax and stop worrying about situations you have no control over. During this waiting time, make a plan of action on how you are going to move forward.

How do I make a plan, you ask? First things first, take a moment to recognize that everything happens for a reason. If you are moving ahead onto another date, great. If not, also great. It may be a hard pill to swallow, but it could be saving you from something, good or bad. Either way, the way it is supposed to happen is the way it is going to go. Don't take that as if your work is done. Even the Bible states, "Faith without works is dead." Have faith that everything will go as it should, but also know that there is always work that needs to be done. In retrospect, understand that life does not always go as you have planned, and that it is okay. When life hands your lemons, make lemonade.

With that being said make a plan using small goals to reach larger goals but be ready to make adjustments as you journey throughout life.

As you adjust, you are going to learn three main components; accept things for what they are, learn how to compromise, and know when to move on.

Accept things for what they are

By accepting things for what they are, you will in turn make life so much easier for yourself. There is something about forcing things; they never seem to work out. Remember you only have the ability to control yourself. I saw a post on Instagram that read, "Consider how hard it is to change yourself, and you'll understand what little chance you have in trying to change others." This was the most triggering post ever.

Moment of truth—I am a control freak. I like to plan everything. I do not like not knowing what is coming next. Needing to know what's next has cost me a lot of anxiety and relationships. I have learned on various occasions that there is no reason to stress about anything you do not have the power to control. You cannot make a job hire you, you cannot make a person fall in love with you, and you cannot regulate a person's actions toward you. Once I grasped this concept, my stress levels lowered.

The ability to accept things for what they are comes with the skill of patience. With technology on the rise, society is changing, and everything is so convenient. However, the act of having patience requires a lot of discipline. Take responsibility for one of the things that you can control, and practice patience, minimize your anxiety, and go with the flow.

Before I went on my first "interviewing spree," I was in a frenzy, depressed, and flustered. I was never happy, and therefore exuded a negative vibe. Looking back, I can accept that I was a Bitter Betty and a Negative Nancy. I allowed a temporary position to take over who I was and allowed it to define me. Fortunately, though, in that season, I learned to accept my situation for what it was and decided to find peace and joy despite my current circumstances. I began speaking affirmations and telling myself that this was not my final destination. When the going got tough, I would tell myself over and over again, that "God did not allow me to graduate college just to be a receptionist." With those affirmations, I began to accept that this was not the end, but just a "speed bump."

It is easy to look toward the future and make plans for your reality. Plans are cool and they help. I know I am contradicting myself when I say this, but in making your plan, also realize that your plan is a rough draft and will have many edits along the way. There will be many "speed bumps," as I like to call them, opposed to the common term "detour." I chose the term "speed bumps," because when driving, speed bumps are not intended to knock you off your course, but to slow you down, primarily for safety reasons. Accept your speed bumps for what they are. Adversity builds character. If you want to be a boring person who has nothing to look forward to, then character building may not be for you.

If you have just one goal that you are trying to accomplish, know that there will be trials and errors. With those trials comes an opportunity to learn from your mistakes and gives you a reason to push forward. Anything worth having is not going to come easy. This will apply to your relationships as well. There will be arguments, disagreements, and so much more. The trials will make you want to give up, but don't. Just recognize when you should compromise. However, there is a thin line between compromise and settling.

Learn how to compromise.

During this journey to a successful dating and interviewing experience, if you only learn one thing, let it be that nothing is perfect. Once you accept that nothing in life is perfect, learn to compromise. However, do not let compromising be the reason you settled. When I took the position as a receptionist, I didn't allow myself to be in a settling position. It was a compromise and a temporary one at that. I decided to change my actions to change my life rather than settle. I decided to work harder for what I deserved. I had to compromise my free time to regain my focus and pursue the job I wanted. I took a fast from social media. Although I typically put a time limit when I fast, not this time. This was serious. I decided to fast until I got a new job. I joined a new church and got baptized. This was a serious life adjustment and commitment. I was tired of feeling mediocre, tired of settling for second best. I made the decision to compromise some of my existing habits and mentality to uplift myself internally and to change the trajectory of my life. The same applies in relationships. There will be times where you have to let go of this to get that. Your "this or that" may be moderate or extreme. The choice is yours and only yours. Make a vow to yourself that you will never compromise your sanity, emotional health, or well-being for someone else's satisfaction.

Know when to move on.

Uplifting myself consisted of moving on, not physically, but mentally. I had made up my mind that I was not going to sit in my doubts, but rather take actions into my own hands. After careful observation, I made a plan. As I mentioned, I was going to fast from all social media and with any free time I had, I was going to apply for jobs. And with any free time, I meant ANY free time. My plan was to apply for a minimum of 20 jobs per week. I was applying for jobs under the dryer at the hair dresser, or the train to and from work. ALL free time was dedicated to my level-up. By the end of the summer, I was going to quit my job and go back to work for a temp agency I had worked for in the past. I was determined not to apply to just any job, but for those that aligned with my career goals. No more just submitting my resume and see where I land because I was in fact qualified to do what I wanted to do. I finally felt that my career goals were obtainable. For six weeks straight, I went on an average of 1 to 4 interviews per week.

Then one day a curve ball was thrown. At the time, because I was already unhappy, I was demonstrating very poor work ethics and it had now caught up with me. I was repeatedly late, and my boss was now on his way to discuss my actions and to write me up. Before he arrived, I called my mother. She was aware of my frustration, but also knew how disciplined I had been over the last month trying to find a new job. Her exact words were, "Go ahead and quit. Do not wait until the first." I was so shocked, but she didn't have to tell me twice. I had a nice amount of money in my savings account and a couple of part-time jobs to hold me over. As my boss came to reprimand me, I handed him my two weeks' notice. I was in the mood to live my best unemployed life and I went to Atlantic City for a friend's birthday and had the time of my life.

A week prior to this incident, I had received a call from a potential employer regarding my resume. Although I did not qualify for the position I initially applied for, they were impressed with my qualifications and wanted to offer me an entry level position within the company. Unfortunately, although it was a good opportunity, it would have been part-time in the fall, and was something that just wouldn't be suitable for me. However, the interviewer also worked for a temp agency, and told me she was going to send over my resume to see if they could help.

After submitting my two weeks' notice, I spoke with the temp agency to discuss my career goals and salary expectations. Less than an hour later, I was called back about an opportunity that not only was exactly what I was looking for, but almost doubled my current salary. The job would provide me with necessary skills to move forward with my career plan. Although the organization itself was not an ideal fit to what I wanted to do, the knowledge and skills that I would receive from the position would be essential to moving me to the next level.

I was at that job for almost three years, and in that time, I learned how important it was to accept things for what they were, to compromise, and know when to move on.

CHAPTER 4: MAKE LEMONADE

This chapter is meaningful for so many reasons. Because of my recent interviewing and dating experiences, I decided to write a book. I know if I can manifest this kind of opportunity in my life, you can too. I have learned so many lessons that I am happy to share with you.

1. You have to fall in love with yourself daily.

There are so many outside influences that have you doubting yourself. When those things happen, check them at the door. Tell yourself over and over again that you were created to be great and you will not accept anything less.

2. You have to be specific about what you want.

If you apply for every job opening you see, you are bound to get into a position that you have no interest in. Like- wise, if you allow every man who is physically attracted to you to take you on a date, you will end up with some- one who you are in fact not interested in. Be clear on your intentions and go after them.

3. Do not let qualifications hold you back.

It does not matter if the job description asks for 10 years of experience. If you like what you see, apply for it. What is the worst that can happen, a denial email? It is not the first and it will not be the last. If I would have never applied for that job, I would not be where I am today. In two years, I advanced my career more than I could have imagined. The same goes for those DMs, shoot that shot!! Again, what is the worst that could happen? If all fails, he might connect you with his cute cousin? LOL!

4. Do not settle.

I could have taken the part-time job opportunity, but I would have been settling, simply to get out of one bad situation into another. I do not have part-time bills, so why would I take on another part-time job? I know had I accepted the position, I would have been back interviewing in no time. The same applies with dating. Do not settle!

Every guy I have dated was better than the last. Date after date, the next guy came with better qualities, fitting within the things that I know I want or don't want. Having to accept change and knowing when to let go is very uncomfortable but there is no growth in your comfort zone.

Now, repeat after me.

"EVERYTHING I AM GOING THROUGH IS CONTRIBUTING TO MY SUCCESS; THAT INCLUDES THE GOOD, THE BAD, AND THE INDIFFERENT."

CHAPTER 4 | ACTIVITY:

Reflection time! A common saying, I hear about life is "everyone encounters a storm; you either just got out of one, currently in one, or one is coming." With that being said it is not possible to run or hide from shortcomings.

Let's take some to time to get ready and stay ready.

Think of a time where you were going through a storm and what was the outcome. If you are currently in a storm, what would you like your outcome to look like? If your storm has not come yet, what "materials" do you need to assist you with dancing in the rain. Journal below. Tough times come for everyone. A good thing to remember is tough times don't last TOUGH PEOPLE DO!

_____

_____

_____

_____

_____

_____

_____

_____

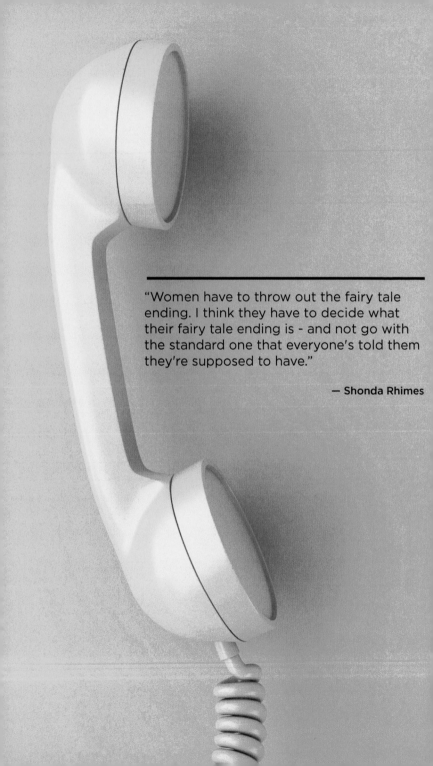

"Women have to throw out the fairy tale ending. I think they have to decide what their fairy tale ending is - and not go with the standard one that everyone's told them they're supposed to have."

— Shonda Rhimes

Chapter 5
The Art of Evaluation

Have you ever sat back and paid attention to the present moment? I mean REALLY sat back and evaluated your current circumstances? I previously discussed the importance of knowing what you want, knowing when to compromise and when to move on. If you have made it to a second date or interview, chances are there is a mutual interest, and this is where you will want to know where you stand on each of these.

Try not to get too excited and lose sight of your end goal. There are still some things that need to be discussed before moving forward. I tend to jump the gun and want to celebrate when there is nothing to celebrate yet. I can admit I have a problem with living in the moment sometimes. If I receive an email about a possible interview, I want to buy a round of shots. Someone may send me a DM and I am mentally planning an entire wedding. (Some exaggeration, but you catch my drift). Often, I have to tell myself, "GIRL. RELAXXX!!!" Just because you made it to the second interview, does not mean you got the job. Granted, it is a good feeling to know you are moving further up the totem pole, but that does not mean put your two weeks' notice in. It means accept the fact that you are heading in the right direction and the things you are trying to accomplish are finding a path to you. The inner work is not complete. Be happy, and also understand and accept that things can go either way.

It is true that believing is achieving, but you have to be realistic with yourself. Give yourself a pep talk, regain focus, and make sure that this is what you want, before you find yourself in a job or relationship you do not want to be in. A wise mentor of mine told me to never accept a job based on salary alone but pay attention to the benefits package as well. Fresh out of college, all I wanted was a position that offered $50k or more. I had a quick awakening when it was brought to my attention that health insurance wasn't automatically included, and I would eventually age off of my mother's health insurance.

When looking for a job, in addition to salary, I would also like telecommuting options, health insurance, retirement plans, student loan reimbursement, and a host of other things. You know? The whole package. I need it all. There are some benefits that outweigh others but all-in-all I am not making a decision on salary alone. Why not look at dating in the same way?

Obviously, you want to look at what this person has to offer, but if you understand what is important to you, the list of "offerings" is much easier to look at. Do not allow things of monetary value to sway your decisions alone, but rather what else of value is there to receive? Money is numbers and numbers will always go up and down or may even stay the same. What other qualities compliment what you can offer them? Going into the relationship, have an idea of what you think you need versus what you want. But be fair, what you require should equal what you are willing to give. Don't have the expectations of making a $100k salary with a lazy and immature work ethic. And don't require the a silver platter from your partner knowing you are not willing to give half of what you are asking.

Take time to write a list of everything you believe you may want and need from a potential employer or person you would like to date. Writing anything in this day and age seems very old and outdated. Why write when your phone has a note pad? Contrary to popular belief, writing lists is good for your health and wellness, and increases your chances of obtaining results. Trust me. There are many studies which prove that writing lists helps reduce anxiety, improves your focus, boosts brain power, organizes your thoughts, and the list goes on and on. Writing lists is a powerful and efficient tool to help you clarify what you want. If you want to go deeper with your writing, rewrite your list with two columns; one with the things you HAVE to have, and the other with the things you can go without. These lists will benefit you when it is time to evaluate, giving you a clear image of what you want.

Now, I am not saying these lists are the key to life. However, it is a great start. Any time you write something that you want, you put it into the atmosphere for it to be given to you. Don't miss an opportunity at finding peace and joy. Recognize your deal breakers or nonnegotiable. If a person or job isn't willing to compromise, then it was not meant for you.

Though compromising was mentioned earlier, it is a technique that is used when evaluating as well. Nothing, or no one, is perfect; including you and me. Therefore, accept the fact that employers and people compromise when choosing to accept us for who we are, and we have to be more than willing to do the same in return.

What are some things you find essential to a relationship that you don't want to compromise on? Whatever they are, hold them dear to your heart. But if you change your mind let it be because you wanted to, and not because you are bending, or trying to comply with the rules of others. When we feel strongly about something, it is our body responding and providing awareness to what's going on. So many people lose sight of themselves out of fear of being alone. Don't ignore your intuition. Pay attention to what your body and spirit are trying to tell you.

I have had my fair share of not evaluating with my best eyes when it comes to both interviewing and dating. I would get so caught up in the moment and embracing the YOLO (you only live once) mentality, that I would forget I have set goals and am ignoring the end goal I am trying to accomplish. I have given so many guys my time, space, and energy that honestly did not deserve to even have my phone number, or know my real name, for that matter. But they were so fun. During self-evaluation I would often ask myself, do you even like this person or what are they providing you mentally and emotionally? Whether they were providing a good time, or the nicest gifts, I had to realize that that wasn't validation to keep them around knowing what I want, and they were not it.

I have stayed at jobs longer than I should have, as well. After checking into the present moment, I realized money was making me stay longer than I should have. I had a part-time job that reminded me of my very first job as a teenager. Everyone complained all day, gossip was at an all-time high, and I was missing out on my social life. I was making all this extra money with no place to spend it. One day, I had a conversation with myself and realized, the extra money I was making was not worth it, and that I needed to budget my spending habits better so that I was not compromising my peace of mind. It was one of the best decisions I made. From both interviewing and dating, I learned that I get comfortable easily, and accept daily routines as normal, and adjust accordingly. Now I know. I am no longer adjusting. If it is not aligning with my goals, it has to go.

Do not allow fear, not living in the present moment, or forgetting to evaluate, hold you back from receiving what you deserve. When things don't work out, I get excited looking forward to what's next. The saying "when one door closes, another opens" is so true. But the part they leave out is that when that door closes, a better door opens. You have to train yourself to believe you are receiving the best version of whatever it is you are experiencing. If you let go, something better than anything you could have possibly imagined is next. Having mastered my abilities to evaluate and self-check myself, I am uber excited to meet my next "upgrade." No more holding on to things that don't serve a great purpose.

1.Step back and really pay attention to what is going on around you. Do a true and honest reflection.

2. Take note on how your loved ones are receiving the change that has come.

3. Check your attitude. Then check in spiritually, mentally, and emotionally.

4. Ask yourself, "Is this meeting my expectations?"

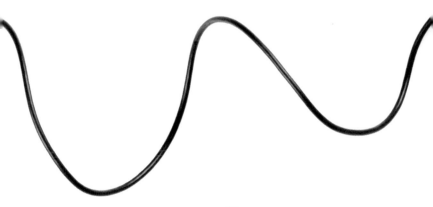

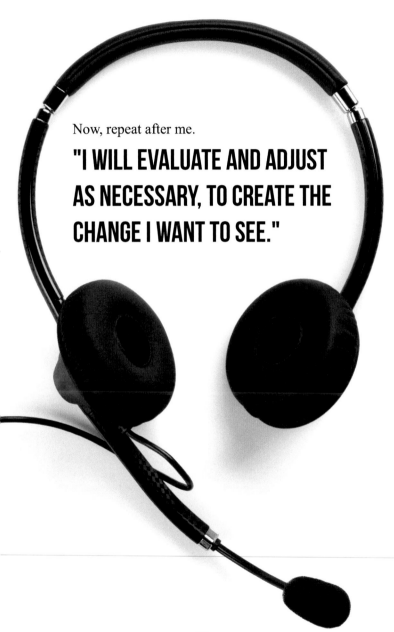

Now, repeat after me.

"I WILL EVALUATE AND ADJUST AS NECESSARY, TO CREATE THE CHANGE I WANT TO SEE."

CHAPTER 5 | ACTIVITY:

Take a look at one of the lists you created in Chapter 1: Let's Be Clear Activity. There are somethings that you feel you need and cannot do without.

• In column one, this should be items you feel like you absolutely need under all circumstances.

• In column two write what you can do without.

This column should consist of items you like but it will not make or break you if you had it or had to go without.

• And column three should contain anything you believe you will not tolerate.

Please
Treat me with highest respect

Maybe
Paid Transportation

No, thank you
Bad hygiene

Remember this is your list for what you want to come to fruition in your life. Do not allow anything or anyone to dictate what you decide is right for you.

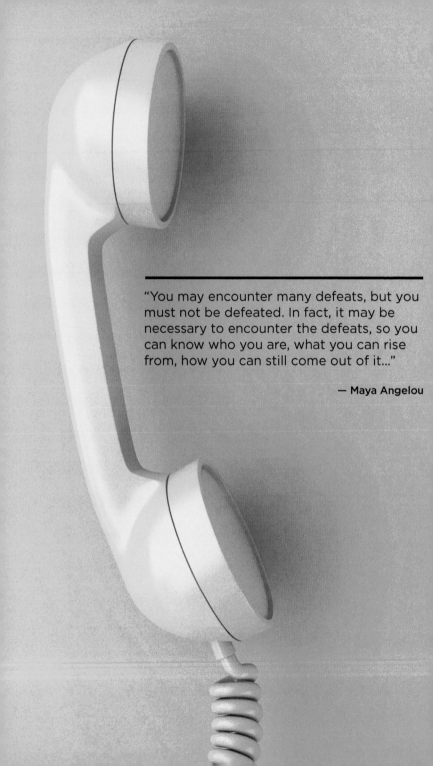

"You may encounter many defeats, but you must not be defeated. In fact, it may be necessary to encounter the defeats, so you can know who you are, what you can rise from, how you can still come out of it..."

— Maya Angelou

Chapter 6
The Rejection

The thought of rejection makes me cringe, especially with jobs. Job searching sure does have a way of playing on your confidence. I believe I have developed PTSD as a professional interviewee. Every time I hear the word rejection, I picture receiving an email including the phrase, "Sorry, we regret to inform you . . ." These emails used to make me so angry, prompting me to text my friends with a screenshot of the "horrific" news I had just received. Until one day, one of my GGFs had received an email stating, "While we were impressed with your skills, we have decided," blah blah blah. My girl needed a pick-me-up. Instead of focusing on the negativity of the rejection, I came up with a more positive spin on it.

I now like to think the word "rejection" is "reflection" spelled wrong. When you are rejected from something, it is actually a good time to reflect on yourself. Try not to pay attention to where the interview or date may have gone wrong, but instead, put energy to where you can improve. Don't let that "no" defeat you but allow it to encourage you to accept it as "not right now."

After interviews, I review the process with my peers that are Human Resource professionals. These same peers assist me before interviews, allowing me to practice common behavioral questions, reminding me to highlight my strengths when asked certain   questions during an interview.

During these practice and review sessions, I am reminded that it is not always about you. When you do not get that job, it may not be that you lack a skill or characteristic, or even didn't present well. The employer may know exactly what they are looking for and may feel somebody else was a better fit. Just because someone is a better fit does not equate to you being bad or worse than them. Look at this like a puzzle piece. Every piece has a particular position it fits into. Just because one piece does not fit at the top does not mean it is not meant to be a part of the puzzle. It just means you have to continue to work the puzzle until you figure out where it is supposed to go.

So, the next time you receive an email that "regrets   to inform you," remember it doesn't necessarily mean you bombed the interview. It can mean a number of things, including you did very well, but that opportunity will not serve you in the capacity you are looking to receive. We must learn to stop taking things personally and/or negatively and use rejection as a reason to get excited to go back to the drawing board.

Rejection is equally important when dating. Emotions are heightened, anxiety through the roof, and anticipation is real. Unfortunately, we live in a day and age where effective communication is almost nonexistent. It sucks that after a date you will not receive that ol' generic email from a potential companion letting you know that they were impressed with your skills but decided to choose   another candidate. At least many of the potential employers send emails and let you know they chose someone else. These days, social media is your best friend and worst enemy. Instead of an email, you see #WCW, #MCM or my favorite, tweeting like there isn't a text from you awaiting a response. If you have gone through any of this "ghost-like" behavior, you have been rejected and it is that individual's loss. Cliché statement I know. Honestly, that is not someone you would want to be with.

Take a look at the bigger picture. If someone cannot communicate with you in an authentic way, they decided to pursue other options, just imagine what else they wouldn't know how to communicate. Keep it real with yourself. I personally have several rules when it comes to dating. I cannot date a person who:

1. Does not possess the ability to express himself in an assertive way and 2. is not honest. First of all, I have a degree in communications. For four years, I have studied how to communicate orally, written, nonverbally, in groups, etc. If you lack the ability to communicate or just do not like to, you are not going to like me because I love to talk, and I am not accepting "Dang, that's crazy," "Yea, I feel you," or you're just being a "great" listener. You have to talk back to me, or I will assume you have a hard time articulating, and that's just something else I am not going to deal with. So please, do us both a favor and ghost me if I have overlooked your inability to communicate because you have a handsome face, or other physical characteristics that may blind me.

Also note, if you do not meet the bare minimum of having a conversation, I will be the rejecter in this instance. On numerous occasions I have served as the one being rejected. SMH. They were such fools, and I am so sorry for their loss. There was a time when I would get mad, sad, cry, throw a fit, and just care too much why someone didn't like me anymore. As I typed this, I heard my third-grade self. Eeewwwwww. But honestly, it is okay to feel some kind of way when you are rejected but strive to reach a level where it does not bother you, not because you blocked it out, but because you are in a self-loving place that you recognize what is meant for you will never pass you.

Rejection is a part of life. It sucks that you and I (and if you are, kudos to you), are not a part of the percentage of people that get every job they have interviewed for or fell in love with their high school sweetheart. That life sounds boring anyway. (LOL I'm hating low-key.) Rejection brings sorrow, but also excitement. How? I am glad you asked.

Have you ever gone to the bar after receiving one of those lousy emails or after that guy stopped answering your phone calls? Or just called a good friend you haven't talk to in a while? The friend that tells you what you need to hear, not what you want to hear? Then you receive a good word that revs up your engine all over again? No? Yes? Hopefully, yes. Rejection gives you a reason to start over. A fresh start is all you need sometimes. It is so easy to get complacent with the current flow in your day-to-day activities. When you find a routine and it works, there is no reason to change. A little rejection is necessary. Adversity builds character. Each time you feel a little rejection does not have to equate to a negative experience. Stop giving yourself pity parties and start hosting meditation moments. Regain your power and practice actualizing all that you desire. Take the time to realize what it is you want from this situation and what you should do to get it.

Step out of your comfort zone. Ask the interviewer what it is you are missing or should do differently to excel on your next interview. Before you do this, recognize no one owes you anything they may or may not respond. Do not overthink this. Remember that you miss 100% of the shots you do not take. A simple thank you for your time email, with a follow-up sentence asking for feedback will get the job done. I have done this on multiple occasions and received great feedback. I applied the feedback to my interviewing routine and became better every time. The last time I asked for feedback, the response I received was long and thought out. The interviewer told me everything I did was perfect and to continue to go above and beyond and express my passion for my career. She also reiterated that they were looking for someone who was more qualified that could jump in with little to no training, and they had found that in one of the other candidates. I interpreted that as this particular position wasn't for me. But I was on the right track. It gave me confidence knowing that my dreams and destiny started to align with one another.

Just because this organization wanted someone that had more skills does not mean all companies do. I didn't get the job because there was a better fit than me, and my better fit was still out there waiting for me. I wasn't missing anything, somebody else was just a better fit, and that was okay. Initially when I first received the rejection email, I was sad. After some self-reflection, I took my own advice and asked for feedback, I was relieved and excited to know that everything I had done was noticed. Also, I knew I did not have that much experience when I applied for the position so to hear that I did not meet that criteria was not surprising. The feedback provided me with relief and confidence. It was then that I realized there is nothing wrong with celebrating an interview. Small wins deserve small celebrations, as big wins deserve big celebrations. If you are good enough for them, you are good enough for somebody else.

A little rejection can take you a long way. If it weren't for rejection, how would you know what else is out there?

It was through the "we regret to inform you" emails that I discovered life comes with "upgrades." As many interviews as I went on during that busy season of interviewing, I received one job offer. One. It took a lot to not give up. After being told "sorry" on multiple occasions, I wanted to take the easy way out, and give up with the intention of just revisiting the job search later. But I had a plan and decided to stick to it. I received rejections and counteroffers that were not quite associated with my career goals.

Instead of giving up, I pressed forward. Never lose sight of the light. It will always be at the end of the tunnel. If you don't see it, you are just not close enough. But it is indeed there. You just have to keep traveling forward until you see it.

I honestly believe God, the universe, or whoever you believe in, tests you to see how badly you want something. If it is what you really want, you are going to fight for it. If it is meant for you to have, you will have it no matter what. Nobody or nothing will be able to stop that. The job offer that I ultimately received and accepted was in the exact department I wanted to work in, providing more opportunity and exposure to help me reach my ultimate goal. Eventually though, I outgrew that job too. But I had to constantly remind myself of all I went through to get to that point. Within a year, I received a promotion to the very job that I wanted and had been striving for. Remember after that interview I went on and the interviewer told me they chose somebody else because of my lack of expertise? The promotion put me in position to receive those skills. In the next interviewing season, I was better equipped and able to move forward with my career goals.

The rejection was worth it. Shortly after I received a promotion with a raise, I worked hard, and got another raise about six weeks later. Hard work really pays off. Looking back, I realized I was trying to walk before I could crawl. I knew what my goal was, but what I didn't know was that I had so much more to learn before the goal became attainable.

Rejection is not as bad as people make it seem. Through rejection, you get to celebrate and learn valuable lessons as well as learn how far you are willing to go for the things you are truly passionate about.

1. Turn every negative into a positive.

When things don't turn out as anticipated, check in with yourself and make sure you process your emotions. Be okay with being sad, mad, angry, etc. Then think about the lesson that can come from this and decide what you can do to make this a positive.

2. Don't take things personally.

More often than expressed, it has nothing to do with you.

3. The next opportunity will be better.

It is an upgrade every time. Not only does the situation or person get better, but you have had time to improve who you are. You attract what you are. When you become better, you attract better.

4. After today there will be no more pity parties.

Do not complain. Do not dwell in misery. Accept it for what it is and strive to put your best foot forward.

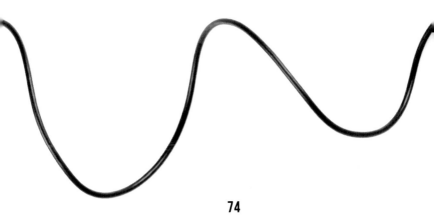

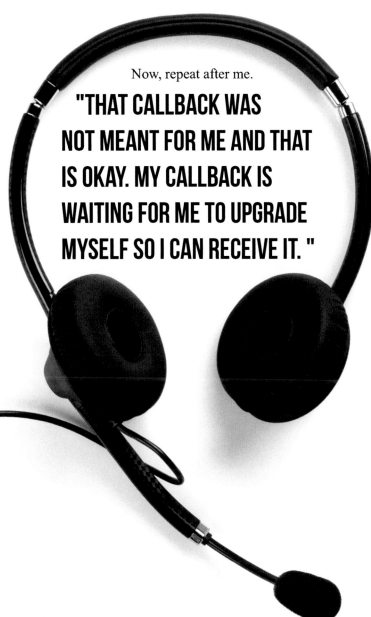

Now, repeat after me.

"THAT CALLBACK WAS NOT MEANT FOR ME AND THAT IS OKAY. MY CALLBACK IS WAITING FOR ME TO UPGRADE MYSELF SO I CAN RECEIVE IT. "

CHAPTER 6 | ACTIVITY:

Rejection. It sucks I know but so what. Let's make the best of it. When I got rejected from that job, I really wanted I was too curious to know why so I drafted a simple email thanking all of the interviewers for their time and asking them to provide any bit of advice they may have to help with my job search. The response is below so you can see for yourself.

Let's draft your email.

Subject: The Callback Intern Position

Dear Jontice Tanae,

Thank you for taking the time to interview me for the intern position on July 19, 2019. I really appreciated the conversation and enjoyed speaking with you about xyz. (Make this personal, nobody wants to ready something you copied and pasted)

As I have great respect and interest in your organization I was wondering if you could provide me with some feedback to assist me with my job search. All tips, comments, and advice are welcomed.

Thank you again for your time. I look forward to hearing from you soon.

Sincerely,

The best intern

This was not much. It was not too long. Straight to the point. Use this as a model and tweak it to your liking. I wanted to provide you with an example to show you it is simple, and it works. If you get a response, please show us on Twitter or Instagram @thecallbackbook

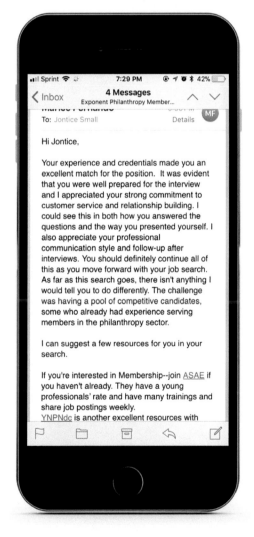

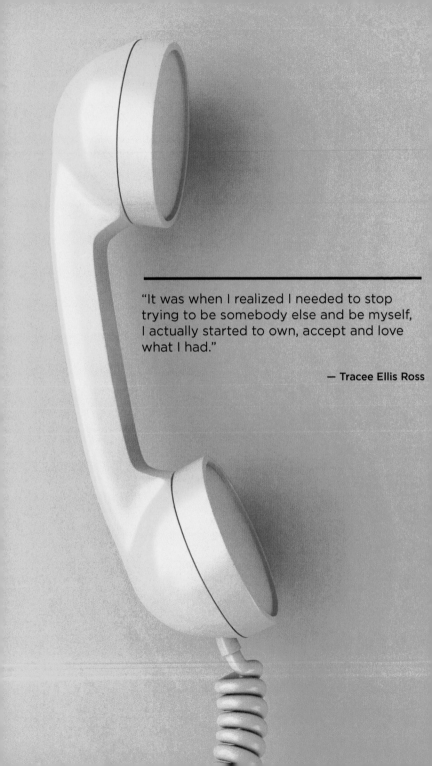

"It was when I realized I needed to stop trying to be somebody else and be myself, I actually started to own, accept and love what I had."

— Tracee Ellis Ross

Chapter 7
The Acceptance

According to Google, acceptance is defined as "the action or process of being received as adequate or suitable, typically to be admitted into a group."

The feeling of being accepted is a wonderful thing. It is something that overcomes you when you feel you are wanted, especially in a relationship or on a job. In retrospect, it is a scary sight to witness the things people will do to be accepted. If we learn to accept ourselves, we should never seek acceptance from anybody else. Accepting yourself and rejection go hand in hand. If you honestly accept yourself for who you are, the notion of rejection doesn't stand a chance. You may think about it, but you will not dwell in it. If you've got you, nothing or no one else should matter.

Being an option or being in the position to be chosen over another individual is not a fun feeling. Well, it may be for some. The hardest part about interviewing and dating is accepting the fact that there is someone else who wants this exact job or wants to date this same person. Just the thought of competing makes me cringe. But when things turn out for the better and the same circumstances you were pursuing are now pursuing you back, how do you move forward? In some cases, rejection is a lot easier than being accepted. When you are rejected, you are sad, but then it is back to the drawing board. An annoying process, but it is familiar. When you are accepted, you have to adjust to change and welcome this new "thing" in your life. It is time to buckle up your boots, sometimes be uncomfortable, and move forward within your life.

There are many voids we try to fill with temporary happiness. For some reason, relationships and job status have become two of the bases by which to measure a person and their success. This really sucks. Just because someone is single and/or unemployed does not equate to being unhappy and vice versa. Contrary to popular belief, that person may be filled with joy because of the lack of commitment. Either way, be happy with who you are today, not who you want to be. You may never become that person, and you may in fact, miss out on the chance of enjoying who you really are.

After all your hard work, and being accepted, a new emotion enters you and you feel the end is near. Whether it was a series of interviews, or a series of dates, the thought of a new commitment is exciting, and thrilling. But it only gets harder at this point. The phrase "hard to get, harder to keep" is real. One of my best friends had a shirt in high school with this statement on it and the immature me never understood what it meant. But, boy, do I get it now.

Once you get that phone call stating they liked you and want to move forward with the hiring process, oh, the joys and wonder that come over you. You are ready to dive in face-first and swim your life away. The opportunity you craved has finally come to its senses and accepted you. YAYYYY!!! Congrats. But before you decide to move forward, always remember to trust the process. Granted, this is something you wanted for a long time. However, do not allow this to consume you. Yes, you do have a fancy new title. But before this title, you had other titles, too: mother, daughter, sister, cousin, friend, mentor, mentee, etc. The list goes on. Don't neglect your old titles for your new one.

Stay the course and stay true to yourself.

Neglecting old titles when new ones come along is common, especially with women in careers and in relationships. We are so passionate about things and people that we put our all into them and forget about everything that helped us get to this point. The secret to it all is finding a balance. Many employers are focusing on a new trend called "work/life" balance. I call it "new" because as a millennial, this term is heard often. But have a conversation with your grandmother or older relative and ask them what their work/life balance was like. I am sure the answers will vary; their social life was nothing like ours today, and some people did not have to work and take care of the home like many do today. When applying for jobs, you may come across benefits including summer hours, 15 vacation days, or telework options (my personal fav). These are ways employers try to help their employees balance out their personal life, so it does not interfere with their work ethic. Good employers want workers who will produce excellent work. But we are people and not robots. We have emotions, friends, family, and other responsibilities that are just as important to us as our jobs. Incorporate cutoff times into your work schedules. No matter how much you have left to do on your to-do list, make a hard promise to not work past that time, if your job allows. Think about this in terms of your relationships as well.

Too much of anything is bad for you. I was told this is in my younger years and did not believe it. One day my best friend passed out at work from drinking too much water. I was so confused. Growing up, my mother swore drinking water was the answer for everything. Your back hurt, drink water; your head hurt, you didn't drink enough water; it's hot, drink water. Water was literally the answer. I bet if I told her my dog ate my homework, her response was going to be drink water. But anyway, the doctors had informed my friend that she was over-hydrated and that drinking too much water can drown you. Do not allow your job or your relationships drown you. This particular day she was rushing, and everything she needed to accomplish that day was done with a sense of urgency. Therefore, she didn't make time to do essential activities like being mindful of the meals she ate or taking a moment to get her thoughts in order to make sure she didn't miss a mark. Had my friend done some exercise, ate some sort of snack, or even drank something with electrolytes, she might not have passed out. She could have done something so simple, like taking a break, or a breather for a minute. She was so consumed with work that she became mentally and physically drained. When you do something for too long and put essentials on the back burner because you will "get around to them later," it has the power to drain (or drown) you.

Understand the true meaning of balance. Balance does not mean to give your all in one area and your all in another. Imagine a scale for a second. In order for both components to balance each other, they both have to have a substantial amount of weight. Then things are added and taken away, so they are equal. To have a genuine balance, something has to be sacrificed. You have to stop trying to be Super(wo)man and learn when to retire your cape. Nothing or no one is perfect. When you try to keep everyone satisfied, you lose sight of who you are. When you decide to accept your new position or engage in a new relationship, remember you will still miss a meeting or two, forget to respond to an email or text message, or miss a baby shower. All of those things are okay. Don't go chasing after being the best director or girlfriend without remembering to be the best you.

Note to Self: NO SELF-ABANDONMENT!

1. Make sure to take your lunch break, unless you absolutely have to work through it, if you are swamped with work, you still deserve to take a 15-minute break   to keep yourself together. Also, do not continuously stay at work late. Quality over quantity. If you have to stay   at work late, pick which days of the week you will, and which days you will not.

2. Still make time for yourself no matter what changes are made to your life. If you have to schedule it on your calendar, do that so you can make babysitter arrangements or husband arrangements or work arrangements. Whatever the case may be, schedule it and stick to it.

3. When you ignore yourself and your desires you are making yourself unworthy of your own beliefs—imagine how others are perceiving it.

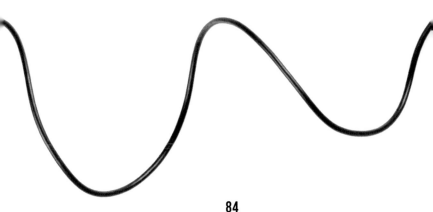

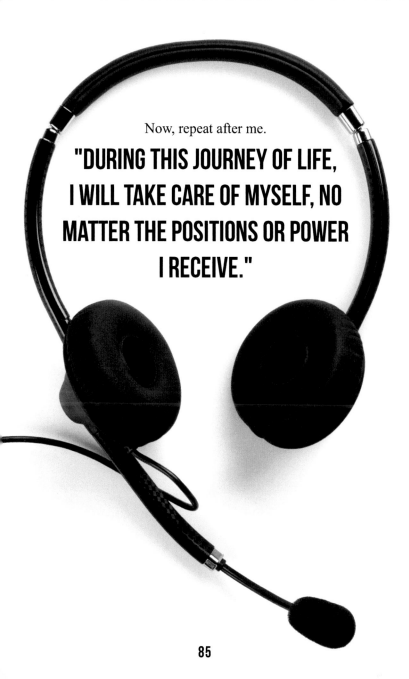

Now, repeat after me.

"DURING THIS JOURNEY OF LIFE, I WILL TAKE CARE OF MYSELF, NO MATTER THE POSITIONS OR POWER I RECEIVE."

CHAPTER 7 | ACTIVITY:

What are some things you been wanting to do but been? putting off because other things are just more important?

Write them below.

Now find your organizer, planner, or calendar on your phone and select your dedicated "me time" days. (I hope you are keeping up with what you have going on in an organized manner if you are not start today.)

Use the space provided to write out your plans during your me time.

Try to do this at least once a month because you deserve to cater to yourself as you do anyone else.

_____

_____

_____

_____

_____

_____

_____

_____

_____

_____

_____

_____

_____

_____

_____

_____

_____

_____

_____

_____

_____

You may be thinking I can't I don't have the time. The purpose of this exercise is to make time. You can't pour from an empty cup. You deserve the best version of yourself as do the people around you. Now go make time to relax and free your mind. I guarantee you will be rejuvenated, revived, and ready to conquer the world.

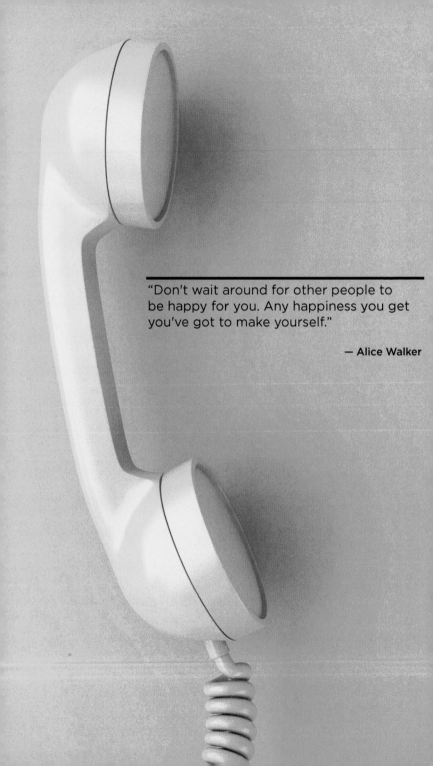

"Don't wait around for other people to be happy for you. Any happiness you get you've got to make yourself."

— Alice Walker

Chapter 8
Falling in Love with your Life (again, and again)

The ability to master something comes from the art of practice. It is often believed and misinterpreted that because you are human and capable of loving, you automatically are in love with who you are as a person. This assumption is true to a certain extent. The notion of self-awareness takes self-love to a higher level. When you aspire to grow to your highest potential, it becomes a repetitive action. You don't set goals and strive for them today and don't look at them again tomorrow. The same goes for the ability to become aware of who you are as a person. Self-reflection is something that you should practice often. Reflect on what you like, what you don't like, what makes you happy, what makes you sad. Just reflect.

Honestly, get in tune with who you are, and what creates your heart's desires. The end goal should be that you fall so deeply in love with yourself that anything a person say or do will not stand a chance at offending you. And whoever enters your life, whether professionally or romantically, should treat you as well as you treat yourself, if not better.

Falling in love with yourself is a practice, a practice that has to happen daily. If you are a person with a big heart like me, you might identify with putting people's needs before your own. Realize and accept that you have to stop being a people pleaser to focus on yourself. Through this journey of manifesting the callback, I have learned to be selfish and to be okay with being selfish.

For some strange reason, there is a derogatory meaning behind the word "selfish." Self-love is selfish and it is okay. We live in a society where it is a crime and a sin to put yourself above others. It is okay if all you want to do is watch TV and lay in the bed all day and ignore all 57,859 messages from the group chat. It is okay to fulfill your heart's desires. It is okay to put yourself first and everybody last. It is okay. Stop sparing feelings. But be fair. Accept that others deserve the same respect when they choose to be selfish. Be the change you want to see. There is a weird stigma on friendships where people feel all friends have to attend every event. That is not right, and we have to work together and fix this.

If you don't choose to be selfish, what are you choosing? Be proud. If you are not right within, how can you benefit others? Stop pouring from empty cups. When you put others before yourself you are being a detriment to yourself and those around you. Some of the podcasts I listen to remind me that I come first in every aspect of my life.

If you need this same reminder, listen to The Friend Zone and SelfishBabe. Both are great resources that helped increase my self-awareness and wellness.

When you reach a certain level of self-awareness certain things in life will not phase you. Those with your family, the issues on the job, the gossip. It will all bypass you because you have better things to worry about. Your focus becomes different, your thoughts become plans, and plans become actions, and the things that once mattered, won't matter anymore. When you reach this level, you have officially reached the level of only minding the business that pays you. Minding your business does not only equate to not being nosey. Once you mastered this level, you will be so in love with who you are and who you are becoming, that you won't have the ability to even think twice of all the things that once were important. That fear you once had to quit that job or build the confidence to look for another one will come. The fear of staying in any kind of relationship because of time spent, will fade away. Peace will come to you and surround you. When you finally encounter this feeling, you will not want to look back. You will join the "protect your peace at all cost" posse and really understand the true meaning behind it.

Once you find true peace and joy, nothing will bother you. You will graduate from the Mind Your Business University and really just do that. Mind your own business. When you are caught up in who you are and what you have going on, no one else's business will matter.

There will be times when you will relapse, of course. However, in this moment, be proud of the person you are, and the one you are becoming through your hard work, time, and effort.

In my seasons of interviewing and dating, I have learned so much about myself. I learned what I like, what I don't like, and most importantly, I learned my limits. I recognize my flaws and strive to work to correct them daily. I see where I went wrong in the past and try my best to not make those same mistakes again. I have learned who I can trust and run to when the going gets tough. Overall, I learned about me and what ultimately makes me happy. There is no man or job that can provide me with the peace, love, and joy that I have found in the process of getting to know and fall in love with myself. If anything, I have learned to make decisions based on the goals I have set for myself. Once you completely know yourself, you will make better, concrete decisions. Your decisions will stop being based on what you think is right, but what you know.

Have you ever sat back and thought about a person you used to date or a job you thought you once loved, and said to yourself, "I don't know what I was thinking?" In fact, you weren't thinking at all. You were just doing, reacting, without any strategic plan of action or research on the person (YOU) that mattered.

I learned to trust the process and understand that everything doesn't go as planned. Actually, most plans don't go as planned. But everything that does happen, happens for a reason. There is nothing anyone can say or do to make me feel like I missed out on the blessings that are for me. Everything has fallen into place as it should, and there is nothing I would change about my past or my journey. Day to day, I try to remember to tell myself, "Jontice, I am proud of you!" I worked hard to become this blossoming woman and I will continue to push harder.

CHAPTER 8: FALLING IN LOVE WITH YOUR LIFE

Think about this:

1. When was the last time you did something for yourself that wasn't a part of your routine? (Hair and nails don't count if you routinely go)

2. Be proud of yourself, not for who you will be, or what you are trying to become. It took a lot to reach this point, and there is still a way to go. Celebrate you. It has been a journey. A journey worth celebrating.

3. Plan an activity alone and enjoy it. Even if this is the one and only time you will do this. You owe it to yourself.

4. Write a list of everything you have now that you used to pray for. Then celebrate it. Congrats. You did it. And you will do it again and again.

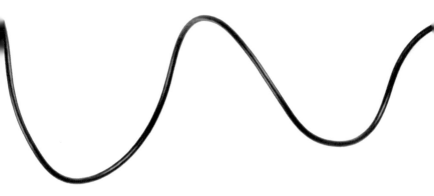

Now, repeat after me.
"I LOVE WHO I WAS YESTERDAY, AND I LOVE WHO I WILL BE TOMORROW, BUT MOST IMPORTANTLY I AM IN LOVE WITH WHO I AM TODAY, RIGHT NOW AT THIS MOMENT, AND WILL CONTINUE TO ACCEPT AND REJECT, TO KEEP THIS LOVE FOREVER FLOWING."

CHAPTER 8 | ACTIVITY:

Reflection…again!

I, _____ (your name)
from this day forward promise to put in the effort to
fall in love with myself daily. I promise to take full
responsibility for ALL of my actions and not allow
acceptance nor rejection define who I am.

I will evaluate always and when life hands me lemons
I will continue to make lemonade. Being me has never
been better than what's to come. I promise to keep it
real and always always always (yes three times) be clear
on my intentions. For The Callback is mine and I will
continue to work on me until I receive it!

Phone Buddy: _____
                              (your name)

CHAPTER 8: FALLING IN LOVE WITH YOUR LIFE

THE CALL BACK

"Ring, ring, Ring."

"Hello?! Are you there?"

"Heyyyy there you!"

Hello Phone Buddy,

Thank you for taking the time to read my book. The journey of The Callback is surreal, and it is my pleasure and honor to share these memories with you. I must say reflecting and sharing this with you has been nothing short of amazing. Oh, the emotional roller coaster I've been on, I wouldn't change it for the world. The tests and trials were all worth it to birth this moment. I hope my journey remind you that you are not alone, and you too can accomplish anything you set your mind to. What you dream becomes your reality.

Manifestation. It is real. So real. As I mentioned previously while writing The Callback, I received yet another callback. Shocker, right? It shocked me too. I was in a funk feeling like I have outgrown my current state and had no idea what to do. I had to reread some of my own work to press forward. Even writing it still gives me chills. This callback was different though. My thought process was different, and I was different. I knew it was time for something new, and I was not settling for anything less. To want something new, I knew I had to not only be different but be better. I made it my business to advance my self- care. It all started with my yoni steam. My very first steam, the yoni fairy and I sat, talked, and I cried as I announced my intentions to the universe. I was so fed up on where I was in life, and was sure things were going to change very soon. The following month I took a solo trip to a state I've never been to before, just to clear my mind, and get myself back to business. As I was planning my great escape, I escaped my then current way of thinking. Instead of complaining about things that no longer serve me, I decided to put that energy elsewhere. When I went to work, I started to complete tasks as if I knew I was going to train someone soon. I even cleaned my desk as if I was going to give it away soon. In less than a month, I signed my offer letter to the best job yet. You see, if you want a callback you can have it. No matter what call it is, a new relationship, job, business venture, sponsorship, whatever the case may be, you have the necessary tools to obtain all those things. Put fear to the side and operate as if the very thing you want is already yours.

It has been well over five years (maybe even more) when I decided I was

98

going to write a book. I wish I would have started five years ago but then again; the story would be different so never mind. What really made me start writing you ask? I am glad you did. It was the day I woke up in the hospital. After a long night of busyness my body shut down at a red light or stop sign (I still do not know which one) and I was unresponsive. The local police found me with my foot still on the break not budging to any of the knocks on the window. The ambulance came, busted my window, and rushed me to the hospital. Hours later I woke up with nothing but a hospital gown and socks on, to a pretty nice nurse reviewing my chart. I could only utter the words, "Where am I?" I literally was confused. The nurses gave me a brief synopsis to how I arrived, made me sit for a couple hours and later I was discharged. Before I woke up in the hospital, I had a couple glasses of champagne, not enough to get drunk, but enough to make me sleepy. I had two hours of sleep the previous night and had worked two part-time jobs that day. I was beyond tired. In the midst of the chaos my only obligation was to fix my window. No DUIs, no harm to others or myself, no tickets. Just a broken window, and some much-needed time off to reflect on what was really going on in my life. It was at this point I realized God had a bigger plan for me than I have lived up to, and it was time for me to stop being so busy and be more productive. Please do not be like me, don't let a series of unfortunate events be the reason you wake up. Wake up today.

When I decided to write this book, I had no idea life would turn out as such. The Callback was literally an idea for two years before I ever decided to put pen to paper. My support system pushed me to exceed my greatest potential, and allowed me to not only produce this book, but also reach another harmonious moment in my life. Over the years I went from being a broke, depressed, heartbroken recent graduate to all my bills paid, full of joy, getting a true hang of adulting, self- aware author. Time AND effort are the healer of all. I say all this to say that I am no more special than you are, and just like I was able to acquire many callbacks in my life, you can, and will, do the same. Life is what you make it. Stop letting people tell you what's best for you Go out there and get what you deserve.

If you enjoyed my story and want to chat feel free to contact me on Twitter or Instagram at @TheCallbackBook. I look forward to speaking with you.

Thank you for your time.

Your fav operator,

Fontice Tanae

ACKNOWLEDGMENTS

First and Foremost

I want to thank God .... for trusting me with this vision and equipping me to bring it to life.

My Mommy and my Daddy .... cus without y'all there's no me.

My Stepmother .... for help raising me.

My Grandma and my Nana .... The two best grandmothers a girl could ask for.

My Siblings

Ayanna, Jailen, Kavon, and Kayla .... for being my biggest fans and supporters and for trusting me to be their example. (As if they had a choice).

My Mentors

Shonika and Shelva! .... thanks for all the solid advice and holding me accountable!

HELLEM

> Thank you for being my muse!!!
>
> Thank you for reading every chapter and providing honest feedback. Thank you for all your genuine love and support but most importantly, the accountability.

The Fabulous Four Callback Girls

Aneshia, Antonisha, Brene, and Jazmin .... from beginning to end y'all held it down. No matter what was thrown your way at any hour you got it done.

CEDRIC

> My bro, My homie, My brand creator, you saw my vision and made it come to life. Thank you!!

The OG Callback Girls

Breezy And Bijon .... all of your time, money, energy, will always be appreciated.

My Big Sisters

Tayana and Ta Mya .... Thank you for showing me what true sisterhood looks like. I couldn't imagine doing life without you two.

Sensational Seven

Forever Sensational .... Thank you for all the girl nights, motivation, encouragement, mock interviews, impromptu therapy sessions. Everything!! It's all apart of my journey and I needed each of y'all to make it this far.

SISTER GIRLS

The prayers the bids the good morning texts the moments of honesty I needed it all! Thanks loves.

KNUCKLES AND VON

Thanks for bidding me to the finish line. The Callback is free! Here it is now, make sure you buy it and read it!

My Brothers

Garry, Anthony, Tron .... Thank you for continuously asking "when the book gon drop", thank you for buying tickets to my events. Thank you for showing up when I needed you the most.

TO MY FRIENDS

Thank you for loving me and supporting me on this journey. I am different and I have changed. I appreciate you for loving the girl I was and accepting me for the woman I've become.

To the readers and supporters of The Callback may my story inspire you to tell yours!

THE CALL BACK

Made in the USA
Middletown, DE
24 February 2020